Praise for *the* NAPKIN, *the* MELON *&the* MONKEY

"A marvelous tale packed with ancient advice that works for modern times. This book shows you practical techniques for handling life's challenges more easily."

— **Marshall Goldsmith,** author of the *New York Times* bestseller *What Got You Here Won't Get You There*

*"A modern parable, with timeless wisdom, to help you enjoy greater happiness and success—*starting from now!*"*

— **Robert Holden, Ph.D.,** author of *Be Happy* and *Success Intelligence*

"In this simple yet powerful book, Barbara offers wise counsel and sharp insight for transforming our workplace disappointments and anxieties into an inspired human passion for excellence and success. If you want to have fun, learn profound lessons about life and transform your entire approach to making a living, then buy **The Napkin, the Melon & the Monkey.***"*

— **Michael Carroll,** author of *Awake at Work* and *The Mindful Leader*

"Barbara's book sheds a brilliant light on the power of empathy and the personal touch, and shows how seemingly simple acts of connectedness can improve morale and engagement. **The Napkin, the Melon & the Monkey** *is a must read for every contact center front-line supervisor and specialist."*

— **Brian Flagg,** Target Corporation, Senior Group Manager, TFS Client Support Center

"The simple wisdom in these pages can lead any organization to create happier employees and more satisfied customers."

— **Ellen Krohne,** Director, Capgemini; and former VP, Illinois Power Company

"This is a special book. Business fables are a dime a dozen. But **The Napkin, the Melon & the Monkey** *is something different. It draws on the deep wisdom of the ages and captures both the desperation and the possibilities of the modern workplace."*

— **Stephen Denning,** author of *The Leader's Guide to Storytelling* and *The Secret Language of Leadership*

"Through her storytelling, Barbara shows the importance of caring and compassion and brings alive the behaviors that can make a difference to customers, companies and customer service professionals everywhere."

— **Barbara Porter,** Vice President, Business Development and Customer Service, Nicor National

the
NAPKIN

the
MELON

& the
# MONKEY

the NAPKIN

the MELON

& the MONKEY

How to Be Happy and Successful
by Simply Changing Your Mind

Barbara Burke

HAY HOUSE, INC.
Carlsbad, California • New York City
London • Sydney • Johannesburg
Vancouver • Hong Kong • New Delhi

Published and distributed in the United States by: Hay House, Inc.: www.hayhouse.com • *Published and distributed in Australia by:* Hay House Australia Pty. Ltd.: www.hayhouse.com.au • *Published and distributed in the United Kingdom by:* Hay House UK, Ltd.: www.hayhouse. co.uk • *Published and distributed in the Republic of South Africa by:* Hay House SA (Pty), Ltd.: www.hayhouse.co.za • *Distributed in Canada by:* Raincoast: www.raincoast.com • *Published in India by:* Hay House Publishers India: www.hayhouse.co.in

Design: Amy Rose Grigoriou

Library of Congress Cataloging-in-Publication Data

Burke, Barbara
  The napkin, the melon & the monkey : how to be happy and successful by simply changing your mind / Barbara Burke. -- 1st ed.
      p. cm.
  ISBN 978-1-4019-2573-4 (hardcover : alk. paper) 1. Success in business. 2. Success. 3. Happiness. 4. Attitude change. I. Title. II. Title: Napkin, the melon, and the monkey.
  HF5386.B889 2010
  650.1--dc22

                                   2009033628

ISBN: 978-1-4019-2573-4

13 12 11 10   4 3 2 1
1st edition, February 2010

Printed in the United States of America

To the thousands of
customer service representatives
I have had the pleasure to
work with and learn from
over the last 25 years.
This story is for you.

• • •

"Work is love made visible."

— Kahlil Gibran

CONTENTS

CHAPTER 1

The Eleventh Problem

I wish I had discovered the secret sooner. My worries evaporated. My daily tension headaches vanished. I began to smile more. I complained less. The little things that used to irritate me just didn't matter anymore. For the first time in my life, I could honestly say I was happy. Happy on the inside.

My relationships changed for the better, too. Jake, my husband of ten years, loved my new, easy-going attitude. Instead of spending his Saturdays working on projects in his workshop, he started spending them with me. Our second graders, Nate and Natalie, stopped their constant squabbling. They were happier, too.

That's on the personal side. My work life is what has undergone the biggest transformation. It's hard to believe that not long ago I was either going to be fired or would have to quit.

What happened? How did I transform myself from being stressed-out and messed-up to being so confident and calm? I learned how to do one thing: unplug.

It all started two years ago. I had just gotten a new job as a customer service representative for Mighty Power, our local utility company. At first, I was really jazzed about the job. The starting salary was several dollars an hour more than I was making as a waitress. The company was solid. It had been around as long as I could remember. And the best part—it offered great benefits. That was important because Jake didn't get health insurance where he worked. I figured that if I did a reasonably good job, we'd be set.

Since I'm a real people person, I figured that a job that involved talking to people on the phone all day would be a breeze. Boy, was I wrong.

One Monday, after working at Mighty Power for about two months, I finally cracked. What a day! The morning started out with Jake and me arguing about money—an almost daily occurrence. Then I managed to spill hot coffee down the front of my shirt. The twins missed their bus because Natalie couldn't find her backpack. And my ancient Honda was allergic to cold mornings, so it took several tries before it finally started.

By the time I dropped the kids off, I was late for work—again. That made three times in two weeks. I was terrified that my supervisor Lucy would notice and put me on probation.

Usually at that time of day there was a steady buzz of activity in the call center. Not that morning. The place was in an uproar. People were frantic. No wonder! Some genius in the billing department had messed up and sent shut-off letters to several thousand customers. Perfectly good customers who paid their bills on time got a nasty form letter that read: if you don't pay up, your power will be shut off in 24 hours.

As hard as we tried, there was no way we could handle the avalanche of calls. Some customers were on hold for 20 minutes! Call after call I was yelled at, sworn at, and called every name in the book. All for something that was somebody else's fault!

I managed to keep my cool most of that morning. But finally, after a string of really awful calls, I lost it. I started to fight fire with fire. By lunchtime my attitude was so bad that some customers were certain they had just had an encounter with the service rep from hell. I wasn't proud of that.

The stress took its toll. Exhausted, I began to plan my escape. I pictured myself grabbing my purse and dashing out to my car. I fantasized about hurtling down the freeway as fast as that wreck of a car could go. The fantasy did not include a return trip.

I figured I was about to get fired anyway. If Lucy happened to monitor any of my calls, she'd be horrified. I would be shown the door for sure.

I simply could not afford to get fired. Not now. We were still trying to recover from last winter when Jake had been unemployed. Losing my paycheck would really set us back. Plus, I didn't want to leave! As hard as this job was, I actually liked it. On a good day I felt almost competent.

Feeling desperate, I knew I needed help. That's when I thought of Isabel. Sweet Isabel. The senior service rep who'd been my "buddy" in new-hire training.

What a woman. She had the most experience of anybody in the call center. I couldn't put my finger on it, but there was something special about her. She had the unique ability to remain calm— no matter what. All the other reps knew that if they had an impossible customer, they could transfer that person to Isabel and the customer would hang up happy.

Isabel had been a lifesaver during my training. Looking back now, I see how clueless I was. I had barely used a computer before. But Isabel noticed when I was floundering and came to my rescue. Now I needed to be rescued again.

I found my hero in the cafeteria. She was standing by the window with her back to me. I approached quietly. "Hey, Isabel," I said, faking a smile.

She shifted her peaceful gaze to me. "Oh, hello, Olivia. How are you?" she asked softly.

I couldn't hold back any longer. I burst into tears.

Pointing to a table in the corner she asked, "Should we have a seat?"

Before I knew it, I was pouring my heart out. I told her about my horrendous day. That I felt like a failure. That more than anything I wanted to be good at this job. But today made me realize that I just wasn't cut out to be in customer service. I hated myself for getting mad at customers who were getting mad at me. I told her I was convinced that Lucy was about to fire me.

My tears kept coming. I sobbed even louder when I told her that if I didn't have Jake and the twins, I'd get in my car and never come back. "I just don't know what to do!" I blubbered.

Isabel took my hand in hers and gazed into my eyes. I knew she understood. She handed me a napkin. Drying my tears, I sniffed, "You're always so calm. How do you do it?"

"Oh, Olivia," she said softly. "I have been where you are." She went on to explain that she had been in a similar situation years ago when she first started at Mighty Power.

Feeling as though her whole world were caving in, she had gone to her mom for advice. Her mother was a very simple woman with a grade-school education. Born in Mexico, she had come to the U.S. in her teens, married in her early 20s, and raised six children. Despite having more than her share of life's problems, her mother had always seemed to maintain a peaceful sort of calm. Her mother's wisdom was borne from experience.

"I sat down with my mother and related my problems, expecting her to take my side and say everything would be okay. She let me tell my whole sad tale, sitting quietly and saying nothing. I desperately needed some answers. 'What can I do?' I pleaded.

"Here is what my mother said: 'For the ten problems of life that come to us, nothing can be done.'

"This is not what I wanted to hear. I wanted the solution to the problems and relief from the accompanying grief. 'Then is it all hopeless?' I cried. 'Are we doomed to just stumble through life unhappy and confused?'

"My mother calmly replied, 'For the ten problems of life—family troubles, work problems and money worries, finding your way in the world—I have no solution. But you have an eleventh problem. For that one I have help.'

"I asked what the eleventh problem was and how it would help my situation. Here is what my mother told me: 'The eleventh problem is your view that you should not have the ten problems. You can never get away from life's problems. Thinking that you can will always make you want to run from your life.'

"That, Olivia, is what my mother told me. It is probably the same advice my grandmother gave her. It was such a help to me, I am happy to pass her wisdom along to you. What you decide to do with it is really up to you."

Wait a minute, I thought. *Knowing I have the eleventh problem doesn't do much good if I can't do something about it.*

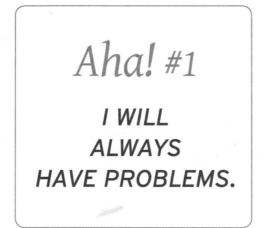

Aha! #1

*I WILL
ALWAYS
HAVE PROBLEMS.*

I demanded more. "Obviously you've figured out how to deal with the eleventh problem, Isabel. What's your secret?"

"It's pretty simple, really. Every day I unplug for a few minutes," she replied.

I resisted laughing. I couldn't believe she was serious! I thought about what "unplugged" meant to me: unplugging a lamp from a wall socket, unplugging a radio, unplugging the headset I wore on the job.

Still confused, I said, "I'm not sure I understand what you mean. Sort of like when I unplug my headset?"

"That's it exactly," Isabel smiled. "When you unplug your headset, you disconnect from all the noise. The voices, the static—everything disappears. All you hear is peaceful silence.

"The same thing happens with our minds. They are filled with constantly whirling thoughts and feelings and endless chatter. I discovered that when I unplugged mentally, it all stopped. All I heard was silence. I felt calm and at peace.

"Here is the best part," she whispered. "I have the power to go to that quiet place any time I want. I can do it anywhere. Sometimes I unplug mentally as I'm waiting in line at the grocery store. When the weather is nice, I go outside and take a few minutes to sit quietly and unplug." She laughed, "I even unplugged the other day as I sat in my car as it was going through the car wash! So, Olivia, you wanted to know my secret. Now you have it."

That sounds simple enough, I thought.

Isabel read my mind. "I have to warn you, though. You will need to practice for a while before you can go to that quiet place whenever you want or need to. I have found that it happens naturally whenever I stop, sit up straight in a relaxed manner, and focus on my breath. The idea is to be present with what is going on at that particular moment. Just relax and observe your thoughts as they float in and float out. You won't be able to stop them, so don't even try. When you find yourself latching on to a thought and thinking about, simply say to yourself, *That's a thought, let it go.* When you spend even five minutes a day unplugging from your busy mind, you will find that you see what is possible and useful. It will keep you from getting stuck in the ten problems of life."

We walked back to our cubicles. I felt a little better. I always did after spending time with Isabel. The idea about unplugging sounded weird, but if it worked for her, maybe it would help me be less miserable. I was ready to try just about anything. I was a mess.

But where would I go to unplug? I needed somewhere far away from the chaos of the call center. Then I remembered there were some offices on the next floor that were used for temporary storage.

The next morning at break I decided to give unplugging a try. I took the elevator to the floor with the empty offices. I tried door after door until I found one that was unlocked. I opened it. The room was pitch black. I flicked on the light and gently pushed the door closed behind me. A chair in the corner was piled high with boxes of files. I placed them on the floor and got comfortable. Recalling Isabel's instructions, I sat up straight, put my feet flat on the floor, and took a deep breath. I closed my eyes.

February 12, 10:32 A.M.

Breathe in, breathe out . . . slowly . . . breathe in, breathe out . . . breathe in, breathe out . . . slower . . . much slower . . . breathe in . . . breathe out . . . breathe in . . . breathe out . . . breathe in . . . I hope nobody comes looking for me. They probably won't. The phones are slow right now. I should be back in a few minutes . . . Nobody will notice I'm gone . . . Lucy is in a meeting . . . When I get back I'll have to remember to finish setting up a new account for that woman in Lincoln . . .She needs a credit check . . . I should go to the bank at lunch. Oh yeah, then there is the Honda . . . I hope it decides to start . . . It is warmer outside, so it should start . . . It must be the starter again . . . I thought Jake replaced it . . . Maybe he forgot . . . No he must have . . . Whoops, I was just thinking . . . That's a thought, let it go . . . Isabel was right—it's hard not to grab onto my thoughts . . . They just keep coming . . . non-stop . . . My mind wants to stop and dwell on them . . . Think some more about it . . . Hang on to it . . . See where it goes . . . This is a lot harder than I thought . . . Whoops . . . I was just thinking about how I was thinking . . .That's pretty funny . . . Breathe in . . . breathe out . . . That's right, concentrate on breathing . . . Slowly breathe in . . . breathe out . . . Slowly breathe in . . . breathe out . . . breathe in . . . breathe out . . . breathe in . . . breathe out (sigh) . . . Mmmmm . . . This feels good . . . I do feel a little more relaxed . . . just as she said . . . but getting good at this is going to take some practice . . . (sigh) Better get back to work. I'll deal with the car later. Who knows? . . . It could start with no problem this time . . . No use worrying about it . . . Better get back to work . . .

10:39 A.M.

CHAPTER 2

The Gift

Wednesday was "disconnect day," the day our guys in the field went out to disconnect the meters of the customers who hadn't paid their bills for months. Without power, these customers had no lights, no heat or air conditioning, no hot water, no freezer or fridge. Even more problematic for many, it meant no TV.

I dreaded going to work on Wednesdays. By noon I had a pounding headache. After trying the usual headache remedies, I'd resort to the old standby—food. First, I would dip into my emergency stash of jelly beans. If that didn't make me feel better, I'd hit the candy machine. Before I knew it,

I'd washed down a bag of M&M's, a bag of chips, and a candy bar with a Coke or two.

Mighty Power didn't like to shut people's power off. We always tried to work out flexible payment arrangements. But despite our efforts, we'd have hundreds of shutoffs every Wednesday.

Many were repeat offenders. To their way of thinking, unlimited electricity was their God-given right. So when faced with being shut off, they would call us to plead their case. Inevitably their excuses were some variation on "my dog ate my homework."

And who would they take their anger out on? My fellow service reps and me. Every call we took on disconnect day was a potential land mine.

"Let them vent. Be empathetic," the trainer said. Be empathetic. Right. How would she like to get verbally abused every Wednesday? See how cheerful she would be.

My attitude didn't go unnoticed by my supervisor. Each service rep received a service quality score based on a random sample of phone calls. While my other scores had been steadily improving, the scores for courtesy and call control were not. I knew that unless my scores went up, there was no way I would get what I so desperately wanted—to get through my probationary period and be a permanent, full-time employee.

My scores were so bad that I was required to meet with Drake, one of the performance coaches. He was a nice enough guy. Trouble was, he'd never been a service rep in a call center. He had no idea how challenging it was to take about a hundred calls a day—day after day.

Drake told me the same thing over and over. "Olivia," he said, "when customers call, they are angry and frustrated with the situation. Most of the time there is a good reason they are upset. Your job is to figure out how to fix the problem. I guarantee your scores for quality will go up immediately once you accept the fact that it's not about you."

The coaching sessions worked for a few days. But despite telling myself, *It's not about me; it's not about me,* I eventually reverted to flaring up and fighting back.

Then there were the daily unplugging sessions. I was failing at those, too. Instead of finding peace and quiet, I was getting even more stressed out trying to control my mind. If the eleventh problem was thinking that I could live my life without the ten problems, maybe I had a twelfth problem: thinking I could unplug my mind for a few minutes.

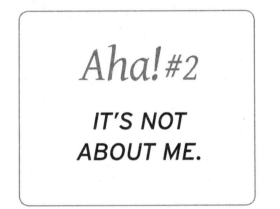

Aha! #2

**IT'S NOT
ABOUT ME.**

Lucy had the patience of a saint. Any other supervisor would have given up on me long ago. Then came the day when I really blew it.

I was in her office reviewing my latest call quality scores. Her phone rang. She picked up. Her face changed from a pleasant smile to a dead-serious frown. The person on the other end was doing all the talking. She listened, took notes, and apologized at the end of the call. "Sir, I am so sorry that this has happened. That is not how we usually handle things here. I'll look into it immediately, sir, and let you know what I find out."

Lucy hung up the receiver and looked at me as if I had committed the crime of the century. *Uh-oh,* I gulped.

"Do you know who that was?" she glared.

"Ah, no, but whoever it was, was not happy," I replied sheepishly.

"Not happy would be an understatement! That was Mr. Mathwig, our new CEO. He just got a call from Mr. Ficcorello, the retired CEO of Great Stuff Industries and one of our largest commercial customers, who is so angry that he is threatening to call Channel 7 News.

"Evidently, he was in Florida for several months. When he got home last night he had no heat, and his pipes had frozen. The electricity had been off for at least a month, maybe more. He said that he called us before he left and made arrangements to have his electric bill paid automatically by debiting his bank account every month.

"The man said that somebody by the name of Olivia had been 'unbelievably rude and abusive' to him. Not only is he calling the consumer reporter at Channel 7, he is suing us for the water damage caused by the burst pipes."

I cringed. I felt the color drain from my face. I broke into a cold sweat. "I think I remember," I gulped.

I did remember—vividly. The guy had called on a cell phone just before lunch. He had a bad attitude right from the start. He even had the nerve to put me on hold several times. Holier-than-thou, too. He claimed he'd set up the automatic bank withdrawal to pay his bill prior to leaving town.

I looked at his account. No record of any autodraft. We went back and forth. He said he paid. I said he didn't. He got angry—and I got angrier. Pretty soon we were shouting over each other. I admit that I had definitely not been the picture of friendly, professional service that Mighty Power prides itself on.

I left Lucy's office in tears, clutching a crumpled, yellow disciplinary action slip in my clammy hand. I wished she had fired me.

Luckily, it was near the end of my shift. I stumbled through closing down my computer, gathered my stuff, and made a beeline for the door. I was in such a daze that I almost bumped into Isabel.

"Oh, Olivia! What's wrong?"

Holding back my tears, I explained what had happened in Lucy's office.

"Let's duck into Starbucks," she said, patting my arm. "You look like you could use something stronger, but let me buy you a cup of coffee." Head down, I nodded and followed her next door.

We settled into a pair of chairs in a quiet corner.

Eyes red and lower lip trembling, I started my litany of woes. I told her how much I dreaded Wednesdays. I told her about my bout with Mr. Ficcorello and how much trouble I was in—with our CEO, no less.

"I'm beginning to hate this job!" I said, pounding my fist.

Isabel looked up from her cup of coffee, paused, and said, "I wonder if it's the job that's the problem, Olivia."

Well, that wasn't what I wanted to hear! Of course it had to be the job. What else could it be?

My mind raced. I tried to think of what I could do so I wouldn't have to face any more Wednesdays.

I know! Mighty Power could just change the policy. They could spread the disconnects throughout the month. No, that wouldn't help. Then I'd have a whole month of icky calls. Or I could call in sick every Wednesday—make up some excuse. On second thought, nix that idea. I'm a bad liar.

Isabel knew I was trying to figure out how to change the situation. "Do you remember the story about the eleventh problem? Remember, my mother told me that we will always have problems in life," she said softly. "She believed that the key to a happy life is accepting that problems are simply a part of it. We are fooling ourselves when we think that we can have a life without them."

Isabel looked me straight in the eye and said, "I'd like you to answer a question for me, Olivia." I swallowed hard.

"If you had to describe what you do for a living, what would you say?"

"That's easy," I replied. "My job is to answer the phone and help our customers."

"And when you are helping customers, what are you doing?" she asked.

I thought for a moment. "I am supposed to solve my customers' problems."

Isabel looked at me expectantly, waiting for the lightbulb to go on.

I thought for a minute about what I had just said.

"I get it!" I laughed. "If customers didn't have any problems, Mighty Power wouldn't need me. I wouldn't even have this job!"

Isabel grinned and nodded. "So you can see, in a way, every problem a customer presents to us is really a gift."

Okay, I thought. *I got the eleventh problem connection. I could see my job was an endless stream of customer problems that I needed to solve. But viewing problems and the customers' anger that comes with them as "gifts" was a big stretch.*

"Did you say *gift?*"

"I know it sounds odd," she continued. "Feeling compassion for people who are blaming you for their difficulties isn't easy. But I can tell you that once I got in the habit of being more compassionate and kind, my job became much easier."

This idea of being compassionate with my customers sounded vaguely familiar. It was what Drake had been trying to get me to understand. I needed to take care of the customer and not take it all so personally.

On the drive home, I felt lighter, almost optimistic. *Maybe there is hope,* I thought. *Maybe I'm not doomed after all.*

Aha! #3

**PROBLEMS CAN
BE GIFTS
IN DISGUISE.**

The next morning I woke up early. I felt energized. I vowed that this day would be different. I was going to try to be more understanding and kind. I was ready to face the challenge of handling the "gift" that keeps on giving—the endless parade of customer problems, otherwise known as my job as a customer service representative at Mighty Power.

By 7:30 A.M. I had already dealt with the endless parade of family problems. First it was Nate and Natalie fighting over who was going to get the last granola bar. Then it was Jake complaining that he couldn't find any clean socks, which led to an argument about whose turn it was to put the clean laundry away (it had been mine).

When I was dressing, I broke the zipper on my favorite slacks. The only good thing was that I discovered a pair of pants in the back of my closet that fit my ever-expanding backside.

As I drove to work that morning, my thoughts drifted to the previous evening's conversation with Isabel. She was right. I had to accept that my life would never be perfect. I would always have problems. I was just going to have to get used to the idea.

I could see that the same idea applied to my job. If we had perfect service and our customers didn't have problems, Mighty Power wouldn't need a customer service department. That was a fact. I also knew for a fact that once I figured out how to deal with customers' problems in a more positive way, I would be a lot happier. And so would they.

Isabel said the key to a happier life was being more compassionate. That meant treating even the most irritating customer with kindness and understanding. The problem was, I just couldn't picture myself not doing anything while people bombard me with anger. A person could only take so much!

She also suggested that I unplug to quiet my mind for a few minutes each day and that if I did, I'd find it much easier to deal with life's problems. I had had high hopes that if I practiced every day, I'd feel much mellower. But no matter how many times I practiced and how hard I tried, I couldn't get my thoughts under control.

The first call of the day reminded me that it wasn't just my mind that was out of control.

Me: Good morning, Mighty Power, this is Olivia. How may I help you?

Customer: You #%&*! people. What is *with* you idiots? You are so incompetent; I don't know how you manage to stay in business.

Me: Ma'am . . .

Customer: Don't you *dare* interrupt me while I'm talking—

Me: Ma'am, you will need to calm down, or I will have to terminate this call.

Customer: Terminate? Did you say terminate!?! Well, you already did that! You disconnected us yesterday for absolutely no reason. I paid you people—I mailed the check on Friday. I can't believe you people—how are my children supposed to live without electricity? Tell me that, will ya? We have no hot water. You have kids? You have kids?!

Me: Well, ah, yes, I have two—a boy and a—

Customer: Two? Well, I have five. Where do you live? I'm sending mine over. They need a bath. Give me your address.

Me: Ma'am, Ma'am, I can't—

Customer: Yeah, right! Then you tell me what I'm supposed to do!

Me: Now just hold on one *minute!* I've had about all I can take from you. How about if *you* take a little responsibility, huh? You say you sent a check—well, I have no record of any check. You were supposed to make a payment the week before, too, and you never did. So if your kids need a bath, that is *your* problem.

Customer: << Click >>

Hanging up, I felt like a real jerk.

CHAPTER 3

From Bad to Worse

The rest of the morning's calls went from disastrous to just plain weird. If I hadn't known better, I would have sworn that all the customers with a screw loose were being routed to my phone.

One guy called sobbing. I got him to calm down enough to tell me what was wrong. He was absolutely convinced that one of our meter readers had poisoned Pooky, his fox terrier. "That guy never liked her," he blubbered.

Next a woman called complaining about her high bill. She was so upset she was hyperventilating. Convinced that we had sent her somebody else's bill, she did an about-face when it dawned on her that her recently installed hot tub might be the reason her bill was so high. Another woman called to say her television wasn't working. She wanted us to send someone out right away to fix it.

If ever there was a morning when I needed some peace and quiet, this was it. I escaped to the abandoned office and plopped into the chair. I hoped that maybe, just maybe, something would go right today.

March 26, 10:28 A.M.

Big breath in . . . breathe out very slowly . . . Bigger breath in, very slowly . . . breathe out . . . breathe in . . . breathe out . . . breathe in . . . Slowly breathe out . . . breathe in . . . Slowly now . . . breathe out . . . Slower . . . I'm not sure if I'm doing this right—whoops, that was thinking. I'm not supposed to do that . . . Breathe in . . . breathe out . . . breathe in . . . breathe out . . . Slower . . . breathe in . . . After a month of doing this just about every day, I should be able to do it without even trying. Breathe in . . . breathe out . . . breathe in . . . breathe out . . . I'll never get good at this. Maybe I'm just one of those people who has such a busy mind that it is impossible to quiet it down. Maybe this is just another thing that I start and can't manage to finish—like all the diets I have been on in my life . . . I've lost count. I lose a few pounds, and then I gain it back right away. I start out eating a good breakfast every morning and even pack a healthy lunch, but by lunchtime I end up stressed out to the point where I am nibbling on something I shouldn't. All of us do that. We kid each other about being afflicted with the "big butt syndrome." It seems to be an occupational hazard of being a service rep—stress-induced eating. Back to breathing . . . breathe in . . . breathe out . . . breathe in . . . Heck, I already blew my diet today when I ate those jelly beans. I may as well stop by the candy machine on my way back.

10:35 A.M.

I knew a sugar fix wasn't the answer. But I didn't care. I'd settle for even a few minutes of pleasure. As I was standing at the snack machine, debating between a Snickers and the M&M's, Isabel walked in. Without thinking, I blurted, "Isabel, I'm doomed."

She smiled and said, "That doesn't sound good."

"I know you said I should try to unplug every day," I exclaimed. "But I can't get it right! I can't seem to control my mind. The harder I try to make it quiet down, the busier it becomes. I feel like a total failure!"

Isabel paused and cracked a smile. "Well," she said, "you have succeeded at one thing."

I looked at her, hoping for some good news.

"That is, you're doing exactly what I did when I first started to unplug. You missed the whole point."

"What?" I felt my blood pressure rise. My voice went up a notch, too. I shot back, "What do you mean I missed the point? Isn't that what you said I should do? Work on getting my thoughts under control? To get my mind to calm down? Isn't that what you said?"

Isabel replied calmly, "You did get part of it right. Unplugging is about allowing our minds to become calm."

At least I got something right, I thought.

"What you found out was that there was no way you could stop the flow of thoughts rushing into your mind. But there was one thing you could have done to get your mind to become more calm and quiet."

"And that would be what, exactly?" I snapped.

"That would be to do nothing," she grinned.

I was so frustrated I could have screamed

Isabel took my hands in hers. "You discovered what I did when I was attempting to unplug from my thoughts: it is very difficult to get out of the

Aha! #4

JUST SIT THERE.
DO NOTHING.

habit of reacting automatically, to latch on to a thought and follow it to see where it goes. Olivia, it takes a conscious effort to stop long enough to be right where you are. To do nothing. To observe *what is*."

Isabel could tell from the look on my face that I was about to throw in the towel.

"I can imagine how frustrated you must feel right now. What you are experiencing is perfectly normal. Everybody who starts on this path has the same challenge. I remember getting so frustrated that I almost gave up. Luckily, I had my mom. I could always depend on her for guidance.

"I believe the reason her advice is so powerful and so useful to me is because it is wisdom that has stood the test of time. The advice my mother shared with me came from *her* mother. Her mother received it from her mother, and so it passed from generation to generation down through the ages."

Isabel paused and thought for a moment. "My dear Olivia, I think this would be a good time to share that ancient secret with you. The picture I am about to draw for you is the same one my mom drew for me," Isabel explained. "I am going to guess that in earlier times my ancestors sketched it in the dust, using a stick." Isabel took a pen out of her pocket and pulled a paper napkin out of the dispenser.

CHAPTER 4

The Napkin

If somebody had told me that a simple picture would literally change my life, I would have told them they were crazy. Now I wish somebody had shown it to me earlier. It would have saved me a lot of heartache and misery.

Isabel flattened out the napkin with her hand. She drew two circles side by side with a space in between them.

"My mother asked me to imagine that the circle on the left represented what is. In that case, what is was my busy mind. Then she asked me to imagine that the circle on the right was me," Isabel explained.

"Olivia, I'd like you to pretend that you are that circle—the one on the right."

I laughed to myself. I couldn't believe I was hunched over a napkin, pretending to be a circle. "Okay," I replied. "I'm the circle on the right, and my busy mind is the circle on the left. I get that. But what about the big space in between the circles? Why is that there?"

Pointing to the space, she explained, "Olivia, that space in between is very, very important. It is the place where your true personal power lies—if you choose to use it."

I had no idea what she was talking about.

Isabel pointed to the circle on the right. "You thought that by bumping up against the circle on the left—the flood of thoughts—you could stop them. But when you tried, you found that your thoughts were beyond your control.

"When you reacted automatically like that, you allowed the event—your crazy thoughts—to control you. You gave up your power. What I'd like you to understand is that the way you regain your power is by stopping for just a moment in that space in the middle—in that quiet place—to observe what is going on.

"I discovered that once I got into the habit of stopping to see *what is,* my life changed. Being able to do that not only allowed me to go to that quiet place, it literally transformed how I looked at my life. It gave me the power to live my best life."

"Really?" I desperately wanted to believe her.

"You'll see, Olivia. Your life will never be the same. It will change you in ways you cannot even begin to imagine," she whispered. "But I should warn you. It won't be easy to change the way you think. After all, you have been thinking that way all of your life. You will need to be patient with yourself. Give yourself time."

"Well, I'm fresh out of patience," I sighed.

She asked a question that hadn't occurred to me before: "If your best friend talked to you the way you talk to yourself—always berating you, telling you you're a failure—how long would she remain your friend?"

"Well, not long. Who needs a friend like that?" I replied.

"Exactly my point," Isabel said. "I don't think you realize what you are doing to yourself. When we talk to ourselves in a negative way, telling ourselves we can't do something, that is exactly what happens. We end up doing what we told ourselves we would do—fail. It's called a self-fulfilling prophecy.

"Our mind doesn't know the difference between fact and fiction. When we tell ourselves something, our mind takes it as a fact. What we tell ourselves eventually becomes a reality.

"Let's take parallel parking, for example," she laughed. "When I was learning how to drive, I had convinced myself that I was never going to be able to master parallel parking. After many embarrassing failed attempts, I gave up. But after several months of being limited to spaces that didn't require parallel parking, I had had enough. I began telling myself that it wasn't that difficult. Most drivers knew how to do it, so there was no reason I couldn't learn. Now I can park my car in even the smallest spaces.

"Olivia, once you start telling yourself that you are fully capable of stopping to see *what is,* it will just be a matter of time before it becomes a habit. But first, you will need to be kinder to yourself. Don't be so critical."

Boy did that sound familiar. I knew I was hard on myself. Jake always told me that I needed to lighten up and give myself a break.

"You're talking about a lifelong habit," I replied. "I've always been my toughest critic, Isabel. Is it really possible to change that? To be nicer to myself?"

"It's a matter of reminding yourself of *what is.* Olivia, the fact is you are a bright, talented woman who can do just about anything she puts her mind to."

At that moment, I made a decision: to do everything I could to learn how to unplug. For the next couple of weeks, I went into the abandoned office every day at morning break. I stayed with it, even though I only got a momentary glimpse of the quiet place. When I did, the feeling was vaguely familiar. I had been there once before, many years ago.

At the time I remember feeling as though I had been transported to a magical, mystical place—a place of peace and serenity. Separated from my cares and anxious thoughts, I felt warm and safe. It was so wonderful; I wanted to go there again. The trouble was, I didn't know how to repeat the experience. I chalked it up as a happy accident.

When my sister, brother, and I were kids, we would spend the month of July at our Aunt Ellen's lake cabin. One warm afternoon when I was about 13, I was sitting by myself at the end of the dock. There was a light breeze off the lake. The only sound besides the gentle rhythm of the waves lapping against the dock was the occasional call of a loon across the water. Feeling relaxed, I lay on my back and gazed up at the bright blue sky. I imagined the soft clouds floating overhead in the shapes of unicorns and castles. My skin was warmed by the light breeze.

The next thing I knew I heard my cousins Tipper and Katie running up the dock. It was time for dinner. I felt like I was waking up from a dream. But I wasn't. My eyes had been open the whole time. I had gone to what I know now was my own "quiet place."

I had no idea how I got there. But I was certain of one thing: I wanted to go back. I fantasized about what it would be like to have the power to transport myself to that peaceful place whenever I wanted to. At the tender age of 13, I knew what I wanted. I just didn't know how to get there.

Recalling that earlier experience, I had more confidence. I decided that if I'd managed to go there by accident years before, I'd have an even better chance now that Isabel had shown me how. One day, all the practicing paid off.

April 12, 10:02 A.M.

Okay . . . Focus on my breath . . . Breathe in . . . Slowly . . . breathe out . . . breathe in . . . breathe out . . . Slowly . . . That's it . . . It feels really good . . . That's a thought . . . It's just a thought . . . Let it go . . . Stop . . . Observe it . . . It's a thought . . . Breathe in . . . breathe out . . . breathe in . . . breathe out . . . breathe in . . . breathe out . . . That's it . . . Breathe in . . .

breathe out . . . Slowly . . . breathe in . . . breathe out . . . breathe in . . . My feet are on the floor . . . That's a thought . . . Breathe in . . . breathe out . . . breathe in . . . breathe out . . . I can feel my heart rate go down . . . ah . . . That's a thought . . . Let it go . . . That's a thought . . . Let it go . . . Breathe in . . . Mmmm, what time is it?. . . Oh dear . . . It's almost a quarter after . . . I'd better go!

10:13 A.M.

Isabel's prediction had come true! Learning to unplug gave me the ability to go to that place in my mind where I feel peaceful and calm. She said that once I figured out how to simply observe my thoughts and not get caught up in them, I would start to see the events in my life differently. Gaining that inner power would enable me to calmly consider *what is* and then decide what to do. I'd be able to be more loving and compassionate. I'd become the best Olivia I could be.

I looked forward to taking my newfound power for a test-drive. I got the opportunity the very next day on my way to work.

Usually, when I encounter a pokey driver hanging in the fast lane, I do what everybody else does.

I hug their bumper in hopes that they get the message to move over to where they belong—the slow lane. If that doesn't work I roar past them on the right, swearing and flipping them off. This time, I did neither. It surprised the heck out of me.

As I merged onto the freeway, I moved into the left lane as usual. I found myself behind a powder blue Buick sedan. At first glance it didn't appear that anyone was in the driver's seat. Then I saw a tiny head of blue hair barely visible over the steering wheel. As everyone else was zooming along at 70 miles an hour, she was crawling along at 30. She appeared to be completely oblivious to the angry honks of the other drivers.

I observed the situation. I could see *what is.* This was an elderly woman driving dangerously slow. Perhaps she had gotten confused and turned onto the freeway by mistake. I imagined how frightened and helpless she might feel.

I remained behind her, hoping she would notice she was in the wrong lane. Finally, after several miles she put her blinker on. It took a while for her to make her move, but she got in the right lane and exited safely. *Whew,* I thought. *I hope she gets to where she is going in one piece.*

Most mornings, by the time I arrive at the office, I am already stressed out, full of negative

Aha! #5

THERE IS NO SUCH THING AS A DIFFICULT SITUATION.

feelings. But this morning was different. I felt confident, even happy. I had finally discovered the answer to one of life's most perplexing mysteries—how to maintain a sense of calm in the face of difficulty. I realized that when I stopped to observe *what is* and avoided my usual angry, knee-jerk reaction, I could decide the best course of action. In this instance, the right thing to do— the more productive thing—was to choose compassion over anger.

I could see that judging situations—and people—as good or bad, right or wrong, fast or slow was not useful. I had heard the weatherman on the radio refer to this tendency as the "Goldilocks syndrome." He remarked that people who lived in the Midwest complained a lot about the weather. Because of the extremes in temperature (from 30 below in the winter to 100 degrees in the summer), the conditions were always "too hot" or "too cold." The weather was hardly ever "just right."

I laughed as I thought about how I must have the same affliction. It looked like the only remedy was learning how to unplug. To stop and see *what is*.

CHAPTER 5

Have a SODA, My Dear

That morning I had a smile on my face and a bounce in my step as I made my way to the cafeteria. I ran into Isabel at the coffee machine. "Well, hello, Olivia," she chirped. "You look unusually happy for this early in the morning. What's up?"

"I have some good news," I whispered. "Whatever you said the other day gave me the kick I needed. I finally unplugged yesterday. It was an amazing feeling."

"I'm so glad, Olivia. I knew you would get there eventually. It was just a matter of time."

Isabel paused for a moment. Then with a twinkle in her eye, she asked, "I am curious about something. You and I talked about many things in our last conversation. Was there anything in particular that you found to be useful?"

I didn't miss a beat. "Absolutely! The one thing you said that I kept repeating over and over in my head was the part about my needing to 'stop to observe, and then decide how to act.'"

"Hey, congratulations! You discovered my favorite acronym: SODA!" she giggled.

I thought back to what I had said.

I repeated it to myself: *Stop, observe, decide, act.* "Of course! I get it!" I exclaimed. "SODA stands for Stop, Observe, Decide, and Act. I like it!"

SODA was an acronym I would never forget.

"Isabel, I have to tell you about what happened to me on the way to work. I surprised even myself!"

I described my encounter with the little old lady on the freeway. I told her I was surprised that I didn't fall into my usual habit, which was to jump to the conclusion that she was just another inconsiderate driver. Instead, I stopped myself from reacting automatically. When I stopped long enough to observe what was really going on, I could see that the woman was in a dangerous situation. Instead of getting angry, I responded with kindness.

I didn't expect my little story to get such an emotional reaction. Isabel had tears in her eyes.

Aha! #6

**WHEN ALL
ELSE FAILS
HAVE A SODA.**

"Oh, Olivia," she said. "You learned such an important lesson from that little old lady. You not only applied SODA when you stopped to observe what was happening—you went beyond that. You resisted judging her. Instead of stereotyping her as just another pokey driver, you withheld judgment."

"You are right," I beamed. "When I did, I could see that the best thing to do was to show her some understanding and to treat her with compassion."

"I used to be very judgmental," Isabel confessed. "That was until I realized how harmful it was. When I started at Mighty Power 25 years ago, one of the senior service reps took me aside. She informed me that it was a 'known fact' that anybody who lived in Terrace Pines, the local trailer court, was 'trouble.' As she put it, 'They are all deadbeats, every last one of them.' Eager to learn whatever shortcuts I could to make a complex job simpler, I went along with her stereotyping. I soon discovered how unfair it was to judge somebody on the basis of where they live, or, for that matter, anything else so arbitrary."

Then it dawned on me. I was guilty of the same thing! I jumped to conclusions about my customers all the time. I had to admit that the woman with the five kids never had a chance with me. As soon as I saw her address was in Terrace Pines,

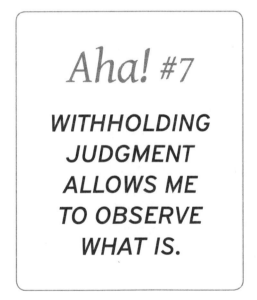

Aha! #7

*WITHHOLDING
JUDGMENT
ALLOWS ME
TO OBSERVE
WHAT IS.*

I pegged her as just another irresponsible deadbeat. I showed her no mercy.

My judgmental attitude wasn't reserved just for my customers. I applied it pretty freely to myself. During my failed unplugging session the day before, I had categorized myself as one of those people who had such a busy mind I'd never be able to unplug. I had decided that I was not only a failure at learning to unplug but also a failure at every attempt at self-improvement.

I vowed to be more patient with myself next time.

I thought back to a morning last week when I had lost my temper with Nate and Natalie. Their crime? Dawdling over breakfast. Their chattering and teasing had slowed down their progress toward finishing their breakfast. I had decided that if that continued they were going to be late for the bus again. I had given them the ultimatum: "Finish those Cheerios, or else!"

I could see that if I had applied the SODA formula to the situation, the outcome would have been much better. Giving myself time to stop, observe, and then decide how to act would have helped me realize that another two minutes at the breakfast table wouldn't have made the difference between being on time for the bus or not.

I needed to be more patient. I had to face the fact that my kids weren't little adults. They were kids. Kids tend to play at inconvenient times and pay no attention to the clock.

I vowed to be more patient with Nate and Natalie next time, too.

Then there was Jake, poor guy. According to me, he couldn't do anything right. No wonder he was so defensive. Being criticized for every move you make would make anybody paranoid.

When he and I started dating, I thought his idiosyncrasies were endearing. Not anymore. Instead of accepting him as he is—the man I fell in love with 12 years ago—I had set out to change him into somebody else.

The problem was that had I actually succeeded in changing him, he would have lost those very characteristics that make him who he is. Maybe if I eased off of the criticism he would spend more time with me and less time working in his workshop in the garage. I vowed to be more patient with Jake in the future.

I could also see that somewhere along the way I had appointed myself the General Manager of the Universe. My attempt to control everything and everybody had to change or I was never going to be at peace with myself or with the rest of the

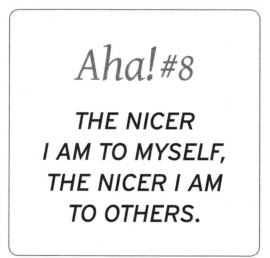

Aha! #8

**THE NICER
I AM TO MYSELF,
THE NICER I AM
TO OTHERS.**

planet. I could see now that once I let go of my need to be in control, all my relationships would improve. My customers would be happier and so would I.

I made another decision. I resigned from my self-appointed position as the General Manager of the Universe. Effective immediately.

I continued to discover the power of letting go. Once I let go of the notion that everybody needed to meet my impossibly high standards, my life got a whole lot easier. I began noticing it when I talked to my customers. I thought it was odd that all my customers were in such great moods one day. Instead of arguing with me, every customer was friendly and cooperative. I had to laugh when it dawned on me that they were responding to my more positive, patient approach.

I recall a couple of customers in particular. Both started out wanting to tear me (or anybody at Mighty Power, for that matter) limb from limb. But by the time we hung up, they were as happy as could be. In each situation the problem was due to a mistake somebody at Mighty Power had made. Both errors were doozies.

Walter had done what he was supposed to do. He had called us several weeks in advance to place his order for new service for the home he was having built in a new development outside of town. Whoever took the order must have transposed a couple of numbers in the address. The result? Our field crew installed the new service not at his house but the house next door. So, when the day came for the contractors to start on the next phase of the project, they couldn't work because they had no electricity. The couple of days it took to get a crew out there to install the new service resulted in the whole project falling behind schedule.

The other issue was our fault, too. When I spoke with Steve, he was so upset I thought he was going to have a heart attack. I couldn't blame him. Someone on our end had neglected to notify him that we were coming out to chop down a tree that had grown dangerously close to one of our power lines. Steve was horrified when he pulled into his driveway and discovered that his beautiful, stately oak had disappeared.

Before my epiphany a few weeks ago, I wouldn't have even considered apologizing to these customers for the inconvenience we had caused them. In fact, when the woman who trained us in customer service techniques had told us that that was what we should do, I had protested. I remember saying, "Heck, why should I apologize? It wasn't *my* fault!"

When I applied the SODA idea to dealing with my customers' problems, I could see that apologizing for the inconvenience we had caused was the right thing to do. I found myself spending less time talking and more time listening. Instead of *telling* customers what I could or couldn't do for them, I was *asking* them questions. I let them explain and didn't interrupt. I learned a lot.

Once I said the words "I apologize," I noticed that the customers' demeanors did an about-face. They instantly stopped yelling and calmed down. Drake was right. All any customer really wants when they call is for someone in the company to listen to their problem and take responsibility for fixing it. I discovered that once I stopped being so defensive, the customer and I ended up on the same side. We worked together to find the best solution to their problem.

After those two calls, the rest were the typical mix of setting up electric service and dealing with complaints. Not one difficult customer among them. At break time I went in my "private office" to unplug.

April 20, 10:05 A.M.

Relax . . . Breathe in . . . breathe out . . . I'm getting the hang of this stop-and-observe thing. I can see how it

Aha! #9

A SIMPLE APOLOGY WORKS WONDERS.

*applies to life in general . . . (sigh) . . . That's a thought.
Let it go. Watch it go, like a cloud passing overhead.
Breathe in . . . breathe out . . . Slowly . . . breathe
in . . . breathe out. Another cloud . . . Let it go. Breathe
in . . . breathe out . . . breathe in . . . breathe out . . .
Thought—let it go . . . Whoa! Look at the time—
it's 10:15 already! I must have gone to that quiet
place again.*

10:15 A.M.

Olivia, girl, you've got the power, I smiled to
myself. Being able to stop to see *what is* was the
greatest power of all. I knew that my newfound
happiness was the direct result of unplugging
every day and applying the SODA idea. I realized
that the power I thought I had when I was trying
to micromanage everyone and everything was just
an illusion. This was *real* power.

Once I shifted my perspective from critic to
observer *everything* changed. Take my relationship
with Jake, for example. Once I stopped being so
critical of him and stopped my nit-picking, we got
along much better. We started laughing more and
arguing less. We were back to having fun together.

I knew Jake was feeling better about us when
he asked me out on a date for Friday, the night he

usually reserved for working on projects in the garage. We got a sitter and went out to dinner and a movie, just like old times.

I found myself relating to my children differently, too. I discovered that the more I listened and the less I talked, the more I learned. For example, I discovered that two older boys on the afternoon bus were bullying Nate. I felt awful that I hadn't picked up on it, and I called the school principal the following day.

I also hadn't realized that we had a budding environmentalist in our house. One evening as Natalie and I were unloading the dishwasher she brought me up to date on what she was learning in school. She told me that her class was discussing energy conservation and the impact one family's garbage had on the environment. We talked about the fact that we really didn't recycle as much as we could. We now have four bins in our garage reserved for recycling.

Aha! #10

THE LESS I TALK, THE MORE I LEARN.

CHAPTER 6

A Napkin and a SODA

April 23
To: Isabel
From: Olivia
Subject: Thanks for the "Aha!s"

Hey Isabel,

Thanks for touching base. Yes, I miss our lunches, too! Hopefully once we get past the deluge of spring calls, we can find the time to get together. Thanks to you I have had some major "aha!s" in the last month or so. Here is my list so far:

Aha! #1: I will always have problems.
Your story about the eleventh problem helped me realize that the sooner I accepted the fact that problems are just a part of life, the happier I would

be. I am learning that while I can influence some of the outcomes by making better decisions, I cannot control much of what happens.

Aha! #2: It's not about me.

I can see now that when customers are angry, they are frustrated with the situation, not with me. And that when I put my energy into solving their problems instead of getting angry back, the customers are happier and so am I. It's taken me a while, but I finally get that "it's not about me."

Aha! #3: Problems can be gifts in disguise.

At first I thought the idea about problems actually being gifts in disguise was nuts. But once I started practicing SODA I could see that every call from a customer was an opportunity to practice understanding and compassion.

Aha! #4: Just sit there. Do nothing.

When I finally figured out that the key to calming my mind was to sit and *do* nothing, unplugging got a lot easier. Now when my thoughts are bouncing all over the place, I remind myself to just sit and observe them. It works every time.

Aha! #5: There is no such thing as a difficult situation.

Situations in themselves are not "difficult." Situations are just that—situations. I know now that when my car doesn't start in the morning, I am the one who decides whether it will ruin my day or be just a minor inconvenience.

Aha! #6: When all else fails, have a SODA.

The "Stop, Observe, Decide, and Act" principle is the key to accessing my personal power. When I started to put the idea into practice, the results were astonishing. My ability to be more patient has transformed my relationships both at home and at work. Everybody is a lot happier.

Aha! #7: Withholding judgment allows me to observe *what is.*

I used to get so caught up in deciding whether something or someone met my impossibly high standards that I lost sight of reality. Once I let go of judging everyone (including myself) two things happened: my relationships improved, and I felt less stressed out. It was only after I resigned as General Manager of the Universe that I realized how much of my stress was created by me.

Aha! #8: The nicer I am to myself, the nicer I am to others.

Unplugging helped me see how self-critical I've been. Once I let go of the notion that I needed to be perfect and so did everyone else, I became more patient with myself and others.

Aha! #9: A simple apology works wonders.

I never considered it my responsibility to apologize to a customer for the inconvenience a problem had caused. But then I tried it. I was amazed at how those two words, "I apologize," immediately diffused customers' anger.

Aha! #10: The less I talk, the more I learn.

Becoming a better listener has paid off in all areas of my life, especially when it comes to parenting. I discovered that when I allowed the kids to express themselves, I was less likely to jump in with my opinion. They didn't need my opinion as much as they needed my undivided attention.

Thanks, Isabel, for all you've done to open my eyes. Just as you predicted, my life has changed in ways that I never could have imagined!

. . .

Unplugging became a regular part of my daily routine. Of course, as an imperfect being, I periodically found myself slipping back into crabby, controller mode. When I did, Isabel would notice and provide me with a gentle reminder. Still, it took me a while to get the message.

That spring we lived through the legendary tornado now referred to as the "Big Outage." Power lines went down in every part of our service area. Over 100,000 of our customers were left without electricity. Even with the help of crews from neighboring utility companies it took us several days to get everyone's power restored.

Every employee we had was called in to handle the avalanche of customer calls. At one point, we had so many calls that our phone system overloaded and crashed. It was a *real* disaster.

Even our new CEO, Mr. Mathwig, came down from his cushy office on the fifth floor to help out. As hard as he tried, he just couldn't navigate his way through our complex computer system. Once he determined that he was more a liability than an asset, he handed his headset over to Lucy. She put him to work delivering coffee and bagels to our workstations to keep us going.

We were so busy the first day of the outage that it was 2:00 P.M. before I could even think about eating lunch. I ran into Isabel as I was dashing into the cafeteria. After exchanging a quick hello, she asked me to close my eyes and open my hand. "I have a present I want to give you," she said.

Hoping it might be something good, I obliged. I opened my eyes, only to discover that she had given me a paper napkin, folded in half. *How nice,* I thought. She must have seen that I was in a hurry. "Thanks!" I said and rushed back to my workstation.

It wasn't until it happened a second time that I got her message. Giving me a napkin was her way of reminding me about the two circles and the space in between that she had drawn for me—my big "aha!" moment of a few months ago.

After that, whenever she noticed I was losing my cool, she'd ask me to open my hand to receive the napkin. We'd both chuckle at our little secret.

My personal transformation didn't remain a secret for long, however. It started with smiling. One day I noticed that people I didn't even know were breaking into a smile when they saw me. It wasn't because I had smiled at them. I hadn't. They were smiling at me for no apparent reason.

When I asked Isabel if all the smiling was a side effect of unplugging, she laughed. Obviously amused at my confusion, she replied, "It's all about the energy, Olivia. You are experiencing what happens when you are happy—happy from the inside. Happy people put out more positive energy. You aren't aware that you are doing it. You can't see it, but other people feel it. When they feel it, they respond to you in a positive way. They smile at you."

Yeah, right, I thought. Talking about somebody's "energy" sounded a bit too New Agey for me. "What do you mean?" I asked her.

"Well," she said, "it's called the Resonance Principle."

This idea sounded vaguely familiar. Then I remembered my high school science teacher, Mr. Mead. He was one of those teachers who left an impression. He had the rare ability to make complex ideas, like physics, simple enough so everyone could understand them.

In my senior year, we did an experiment in class using two tuning forks. Mr. Mead demonstrated that by striking one tuning fork, he could get both tuning forks to vibrate, at precisely the same moment. He explained that it was because they were tuned to the same frequency.

I asked Isabel if that was the principle she was talking about. "That's it, exactly," she grinned. "You have many different frequencies or vibrations in you all the time. If you project a good vibration, then others will resonate at the same frequency.

"The reverse is also true," she explained.

My teammate Nikki was someone who seemed to be tuned to a negative frequency. She was rarely happy. Mostly she was disagreeable and complained a lot.

In fact, the rest of the team gave Nikki the nickname "Miss Grumpy." She was also the worst performer on our team. Her chronically low scores for call quality brought the score for our whole team down. We had the dubious distinction of being the only team to come in dead last six months in a row.

As for me, my performance scores were steadily improving. In fact, my scores for courtesy and call control exceeded the standard. I had to give the credit to my discovery of SODA. I found that the brief millisecond it took for me to stop and observe what was going on—to remain in that space in the middle—gave me the power I needed to see the situation more clearly.

Aha! #11

**PEOPLE HARMONIZE
WHEN THEY ARE
TUNED TO THE
SAME FREQUENCY.**

Now when an irate customer called, I just let them vent. Instead of getting angry back, I tried to put myself in their shoes. "She is really angry," I said to myself. "I would be, too."

I noticed something else. Being more calm and collected allowed me to come up with the best possible solutions for my customers. They really appreciated the extra effort. I even received my first fan letter.

When our CEO showed up at my workstation, I almost fainted. Mr. Mathwig introduced himself, shook my hand, and asked if I had a minute. I nodded numbly, thinking the worst.

"Olivia, I am here to present you with a letter I received today from one of our customers." I immediately thought of Mr. Ficcorello, the angry customer with the burst pipes. I held my breath.

"The letter is from Sigrid Johansen," he continued. "She wanted to make sure that I knew, as head of the company, what a 'gem' of a customer service representative you are."

"I'm not sure what you did," he grinned. "But whatever you did to make her such a fan—keep doing it."

I resumed breathing.

When he noticed the picture on my desk, he asked me about Jake and the twins. He seemed genuinely interested. As he started to leave, he suddenly stopped. "You aren't by any chance the same Olivia that Mr. Ficcorello was so fond of?" he chuckled. Looking down at my shoes, I said sheepishly, "Guilty as charged."

I hoped that Lucy had received a copy of that letter. My performance review was coming up, and I needed all the help I could get. There was a lot on the line. If I met or exceeded the performance standard, I'd get a raise in pay and qualify for all the benefits that come with being a permanent employee.

And if I failed, I'd be back to waitressing.

I was confident that my performance ratings in the last several months were much better than they were when I started. I just didn't know if my dreadful showing during the first few months would hurt my chances.

I arrived in Lucy's office at the scheduled time and took a seat. Instead of sitting behind her desk, she came around and settled into the chair next to me. I liked that. It made me feel less like an underling. That was Lucy's style.

She always told us that her job as our supervisor was to provide leadership and give us the support we needed so we could do the best possible job for our customers. The sign in her office summed up her management philosophy:

Great Supervisors Do Two Things:

1. Follow the Golden Rule: "Treat others as you would like to be treated."

2. Do the right thing.

I tried to read Lucy's mood by the expression on her face. I was encouraged. She was smiling— big time!

She said, "Olivia, I cannot believe the change in you over the last few months. You've gone from having some of the worst scores on your inter-actions with customers to having some of the best in the entire call center. In fact, your scores are consistently in the top ten."

She continued, still smiling, "Your whole at-titude has changed. You smile more. You are much more easygoing. If I didn't know better, I would think there was a different person sitting next to me.

"I have to ask you, Olivia. What is your secret?"

Aha! #12

**GREAT SUPERVISORS
FOLLOW THE
GOLDEN RULE AND
DO THE RIGHT THING.**

I didn't quite know what to say. Should I tell her the "new me" was the result of learning to unplug and apply SODA to my life? Was she the type of person who would consider that a weird explanation? If I did tell her, would she laugh me out of her office?

I sure hoped not.

CHAPTER 7

More Than One Big Surprise

I did tell Lucy how it had all started several months ago, when I was at my wit's end. I had sought out Isabel for advice, hoping to get some answers.

I told her the story Isabel shared with me about the eleventh problem. I told her of Isabel's suggestion that I learn how to unplug my mind. And I told her that I'd been doing just that every day. I even told her about SODA, and I was shocked by her reaction.

Lucy chuckled. "I am not surprised that Isabel shared her wisdom with you. She told me that same story—right when I needed it.

"Mighty Power was in the middle of its third complete reorganization. The first one had been a disaster. The second one tried to repair the damage from the first one, but that didn't work either. We were on our third CEO in three years.

"A whole new management team came in and required all the employees to reapply for their jobs. Every employee in the company had to actually go through interviews for the very jobs that they had held for years. A lot of good people left because they couldn't handle the changes.

"And then there was Terry the Tyrant, the supervisor of this area. He had the charming habit of yelling at us for every little thing. We never once heard him utter a 'thank you' for all of our hard work. Instead, we'd get a constant barrage of criticism. For Terry, it was always about what was wrong and needed to change. Everyone who worked for him lived in fear of his next tirade. If there is such a thing as a collective nervous breakdown, our department was on the verge of having one.

"I was letting all the craziness at work get to me. I was so depressed that getting out of bed each morning was nearly impossible. I even had my resignation letter ready. Fortunately, Isabel shared her mother's story of the eleventh problem at the perfect moment. That story helped me put things in perspective. It made me realize that I would always have problems. I needed to get over it, get on with it, and get through it.

"Isabel's advice about unplugging once a day to quiet my mind and see *what is* was the best advice anyone has ever given me. After a while, I began seeing the situation with Terry completely differently. Instead of reacting emotionally to his outbursts, I decided that I would just stop to observe the situation. I knew that while I couldn't control his behavior, I could control how I chose to react to it.

"A funny thing happened: I actually began feeling sorry for the guy. He was a miserable, unhappy man.

"Luckily, I stuck it out because Terry was transferred out of the department the following year—"

"And you got the supervisor's job," I said, finishing her sentence.

"Olivia, it is my turn to share a little secret with you," she continued. "I unplug too, but I do it here in my office. I shut my door for a few minutes every day so I can put things into perspective. Unplugging has become my secret weapon for dealing with all the problems that come my way. And believe me, as a supervisor in a call center, I have more than my share."

So! I wasn't the only one that Isabel had introduced to the idea of unplugging. I began to wonder how many of us were making unplugging a part of our day.

I couldn't resist asking Lucy the question. "Did Isabel, by any chance, draw you a picture of two circles with a space in between?"

Not missing a beat, Lucy rose from her chair, went around her desk, reached into the middle drawer, and pulled out a napkin. Sure enough, there it was—her napkin with the same picture.

"You know, there is another thing that Isabel does that has really helped me," she continued. "She has the uncanny ability to read me and know when I'm feeling off center. That is when a napkin magically appears on my chair."

Isabel strikes again, I thought. Isabel is the Napkin Fairy, going around and distributing napkins at that perfect, teachable moment. They are gentle reminders for us to stop and observe *what is*.

Eventually, Lucy and I got back to the reason for our meeting. She showed me my performance reports. My scores, indeed, were among the highest in the call center.

Lucy offered me a permanent position as a customer service representative with Mighty Power.

I accepted.

Then she dropped another bomb.

"Olivia," she began, "I would like to discuss something else with you."

Oh boy, I thought. *I can't take another surprise.*

"I've noticed how helpful you've been to our latest class of new hires. I really appreciate you going out of your way to make them feel welcome. The tips you have offered have made learning this complicated job much easier for them."

I wondered where this was going.

"You know, Melanie is planning to go on maternity leave for six months. Would you be interested in filling her spot as team leader temporarily, until she returns?"

"Well . . . I don't know." I stuttered. "Do you really . . . uh . . . think that I am ready for something like this? I've never had a job with that kind of responsibility before. I wouldn't know what to do."

"I am aware of that, but I think you are ready," she replied. "I wouldn't have asked you if I didn't think you could do the job. It's a chance for you to stretch a bit. Plus, it's only for six months."

Stretch, I thought. *What an understatement.*

Our team's performance was the absolute worst. Coming in dead last, month after month, was downright embarrassing.

There was an explanation for our dismal show-ing. We had more new employees than the other teams, and no matter how hard they tried, they still made many errors.

We also had a couple of people who were close to retirement. They had come from jobs in the back office where they did mostly paperwork and had very little phone contact with customers. Now it was the other way around, and they weren't so great with customers.

I shared my theory as to why my team was performing so poorly. Lucy agreed and added one other thing. "I think the other factor impacting your team's performance is that they don't have any team spirit. I'm sure you've noticed it. Your fellow teammates don't help each other like the better teams do. Instead of having a spirit of coop-eration, they bicker and place blame.

"I know the situation looks bleak, Olivia. But I am confident that you have what it takes to turn your team around. You have to trust that I wouldn't ask you if I didn't think you could do the job. Would you be willing to give it a try?"

I trusted Lucy, but I wasn't sure if I could trust myself. I told her I was honored by her offer but that I'd have to sleep on it. I promised to let her know my answer the next day.

As with any big decision, I consulted my best friend, Jake. I knew that I could always trust my husband to give me his honest, unvarnished opinion. I haven't always liked the answer, but I respected it nonetheless. He would never steer me wrong.

That evening, after we put the kids to bed, we sat down together at our kitchen table. The same kitchen table we've had since our first year of marriage. Through the years it had survived multiple moves, thousands of meals, and scads of homework. It's been the scene of more late-night conversations than I can count.

I filled him in on everything Lucy had said during my review. I felt so proud as I told him I was an official employee of Mighty Power. Complete with benefits.

"Sweetie," he kissed my hand. "I had no doubt you'd pass with flying colors. When you set your mind to something, there is no stopping you."

Then I told him how surprised I was that Lucy unplugged regularly, too. He wasn't surprised about that either.

When I told him about Lucy's offer, he said, "You're going to take it, aren't you?" as if the decision was a no-brainer.

"I'm thinking about it," I replied. "I'd really like to, but I just don't know if I can do it. I've never done anything like that before."

Jake is a coach at heart. "Olivia, you've got to give it a try. Remember, you need to be in the game in order to win. One hundred percent of the shots you don't take, you won't get.

"It's your decision. You can do what you want. You always do," he smiled. "But it is a great opportunity for you to spread your wings. Honey, you are definitely up to the task. You can't help but succeed."

My husband was truly the wind beneath my wings.

Aha! #13

SPREADING MY WINGS IS THE ONLY WAY TO FLY.

CHAPTER 8

The Fighting Melons

The following morning I accepted the temporary position as the leader of my team, The Generators. Lucy congratulated me, wished me luck, and sent me on my way. I knew I'd need more than luck to get my team out of the doldrums.

I opened the meeting by calmly explaining the problem. I showed my team the reports, comparing our performance to that of the five other teams. I told them that I was confident that we had the collective talent to be the top team, if we focused on the right things.

Actually, that was wishful thinking on my part. I wasn't all that confident we could make it to the top. I knew I would do everything in my power to get us there. My biggest challenge would be getting those 12 people to work together.

I went on to explain the reason for the meeting. I told them that I wanted to have an honest discussion about what we could do to improve our performance.

That's when the floodgates opened. Out came a torrent of pent-up anger, resentment, and mean-spirited comments.

Mostly what I heard was how much they didn't like working with each other. Latisha set the tone, informing Pam, who sat in the cube across from her, that her voice was so loud and obnoxious that she couldn't hear herself think. Pam retaliated by telling Latisha that if she would show up for work on time everybody else wouldn't be stuck covering her calls. Speaking of attendance, Kari pointed out, if everybody would come back from their breaks on time, we'd be able to meet the service level standards without any problem.

No meeting would be complete without Nikki, a.k.a. Miss Grumpy, offering her opinion on what was wrong. She accused the poor new hires of not working hard enough to get up to speed. She made it clear that she was tired of answering their endless questions and having to babysit them.

In spite of the initial squabbling, by the end of the meeting we did manage to agree on our goals for the next two weeks. Everyone vowed to arrive on time for his or her shift and come back from break and lunch when they were supposed to.

I was encouraged. But I knew we were a long way from being a team. I would make every effort to be a good role model. I would do my best to live up to the sign in Lucy's office—follow the Golden Rule and do the right thing. But that wouldn't be enough. Unless my teammates stopped sniping at each other, we were doomed.

The next time I ran into Isabel, I asked her something that had been on my mind for quite a while.

"Isabel," I said. "I hope this isn't getting too personal. You've been at Mighty Power for such a long time, and you're one of the best reps we have. Why haven't you moved up to supervisor?"

"Ah, yes. That question," she smiled. She must have heard it before. "I appreciate the compliment, Olivia. Over the years I have been invited to apply for other jobs in the company.

"I know most people think that if you've been with a company for many years, you eventually move up the ladder. But I decided to choose a different path. Olivia, I absolutely love being a customer service representative. Serving customers, I believe, is a noble calling. In fact, I think we have the most important job in the company—caring for our customers. Not everyone is cut out for the job. But those who are, are richly rewarded."

I smiled. I'd glimpsed some of those rewards recently.

"You know," she whispered. "Sometimes I feel almost guilty about how much pleasure I get from my job. I have discovered that when I extend even the smallest kindness, I am repaid 100 times over. That is why I have chosen to remain a customer service representative."

"Clearly you have a gift for connecting with our customers. They love you," I replied. "Like you, my teammates want to serve our customers and be great service representatives, but I'm worried. If they can't be more patient and kind to each other, how will they ever be able to show compassion for their customers?"

"I understand the problem," Isabel replied. "Our family was in a similar situation. All nine of us—my mom and dad, my five brothers and sisters, my maternal grandmother, and I—lived in a tiny house with only one bathroom.

"When I was about seven, my grandmother's sister, my Great Aunt Vera, came for a visit. It didn't take long before the constant bickering and nitpicking between my brothers and sisters got on her nerves.

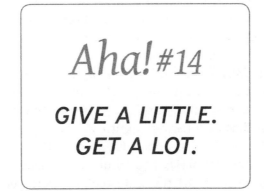

Aha! #14

**GIVE A LITTLE.
GET A LOT.**

"One night as we were finishing dinner, she tapped her glass with her spoon to get our attention. She waited patiently until our usual dinnertime commotion subsided. Without a word of introduction, she proceeded to tell us a story. That story helped us see ourselves clearly. Everything changed after that.

"The story went like this: Once upon a time there was a farmer who was known for miles around for raising the largest and sweetest watermelons. One year, his garden was blessed with abundant rainfall and plenty of sunshine. As his melons grew larger and larger—the biggest ever— he heard disturbing noises coming from his melon patch. The melons were fighting!

"The farmer dropped his hoe and hurried to the patch. 'What is the trouble?' he exclaimed. A riot ensued. All the watermelons were yelling, screaming, and blaming each other. The noise was deafening.

"He looked over his melon patch with new eyes. He could see the problem. Ideal growing conditions had produced melons of unusually large size. The result? The melons were so huge they were bumping up against each other.

"The farmer wondered, *What can I do? How can I restore peace to my melon patch?* He thought and thought until he came upon a solution.

"After several attempts to quiet the melons so he could speak, they finally stopped screaming. He had their full attention.

"'Oh, my beautiful melons, I am so sorry for your troubles. But I am afraid that I am not the one to settle your arguments.'

"This time the outcry was even louder.

"'But I know of something you can do to end your conflict. I guarantee that if each of you follows my instructions, you will live in harmony forever.'

"With that, the melons became very quiet. They were ready to hear what they could do to end their suffering.

"'I'd like you to feel what you have at the top of your body,' he instructed. The melons did as the farmer asked and looked at him, expecting something more than the obvious. Of course, there was a vine sticking out on top.

"'Now, my dear melons, I'd like you to follow that vine to its end.' The melons obeyed and traced the vine, past the many leaves. 'Keep going,' the farmer encouraged. 'Keep going until you find the end of your vine.'

"All of a sudden there was dead silence. A soft, collective sigh rose from the patch. The melons had discovered that they were all one plant.

Aha! #15

**REMEMBER,
WE ALL SHARE
THE SAME VINE.**

"From that day forward, the melons lived in peace and harmony. They grew to record size and won many awards at the county fair that year. Everyone agreed that the farmer's melons were the biggest and the sweetest."

That is the perfect story for my situation, I thought. Just like the melons, if my team could stop yelling "Me! Me! Me!" and start accommodating each other, we could achieve great things.

The power of a story was something I had experienced after attending a storytelling workshop sponsored by my church. The workshop facilitator, Paul, was a terrific storyteller. He had a way of telling a story that kept us on the edge of our seats, wanting to know what came next. The story he told was about the most influential man in his life—his dad. He managed to have us laughing and crying in the span of a few minutes.

After sharing his story, he gave us some pointers on how to tell a compelling story. Our assignment, he said, was to share our own story. Each of us was to talk about the most influential person in our lives.

As we went around the circle, each of us told our personal story. We learned about the struggles, passions, and turning points in our lives. We learned more about each other in the ten minutes it took for each of us to tell our stories than if we had attended 100 Sunday services together.

We started off our next team meeting by reviewing the previous week's performance scores. Finally, there was good news to report. "You all did great this week!" I exclaimed. "We have already seen an improvement in our scores. If we continue to adhere to our schedule, we should see even more progress. But we still have one important issue we need to address," I said.

Nikki raised her hand. "Only one? I can think of 100."

"You're right," I replied. "We do have several important issues to deal with. But, frankly, if we can't manage to solve our number one problem, we'll never get out of last place."

I could tell by the blank look on their faces that they had no idea what I was referring to.

"But before we discuss that, I'd like to share a little story with you that I think illustrates our problem. As you listen, I'd like you to consider whether this story parallels our team's situation."

I told the story of the fighting melons. When I finished, I could see everyone was smiling. They got it!

Audry shot up her hand. "I like it! You nailed it, Olivia. That is exactly what we've been doing—bumping up against each other."

Megan, one of the new hires, piped up, "I think we are going to have to stop squabbling and concentrate on working together. I've seen what happens when people can't put their differences aside and work together. At my last job, the two brothers who owned the company spent so much time arguing about who was right that they lost sight of why they were in business in the first place. By the time they realized how much damage they had done, it was too late. The company ended up going out of business, and I was out of a job."

Lorraine spoke next. She had been with Mighty Power for 35 years. "But Mighty Power would never get to the point of laying off people. We've never had a layoff in our 50-year history. We are a utility. We are a monopoly. Where else are our customers going to get their electricity?"

I was surprised at what came next. "Ah, but not for long," Nikki warned. "We have to recognize that some time in the next few years our customers will have a choice of utilities. Our company will be just one of several to choose from. If we don't clean up our act and start doing everything humanly possible to satisfy our customers, Mighty

Power will meet the same fate as the dinosaurs. We will become extinct."

Jason, one of our new hires, jumped up and scribbled something on the white board. It read, "United we stand. Divided we fall."

That said it all.

"I have an idea," I said. "Did you enjoy the story of the fighting melons?"

They nodded.

"What if we each come up with a story of our own?" They looked at me as if they hadn't heard me correctly.

"You are going to have to trust me on this. I know it won't appear to make any sense at first. But I promise, it will." I said reassuringly.

"For our next meeting, I'd like each of you to answer the question, *Which one person has had the greatest influence on my life?* Explain the impact that individual has had on the person you are today."

I went on to explain. "When you stop to consider it, every one of us has had a person who has inspired us, encouraged us, or served as a role model. That person could be a teacher, a relative, a neighbor, or even a famous person."

I decided to share my story as an example. I talked about how, when I was a kid, my father wasn't around much. But there was one person I

Aha! #16

UNITED WE STAND.
DIVIDED WE FALL.

could always count on—my Uncle John. He had been injured in the Vietnam War and was confined to a wheelchair. He had a lot to be unhappy about, but he was the most positive person I had ever met.

Uncle John always had time to listen to my little-girl woes and give me an encouraging word. I remembered spending countless hours on his back porch, sipping lemonade and talking. I'd walk home happy and confident. He made me feel capable of doing just about anything. He died a few years ago, but I still remember the pet name he had for me—"Lovely Olivia."

We spent the next team meeting telling stories. It was a truly amazing experience.

We learned that Angie had been orphaned when she was five after her parents died in a terrible car crash. Her most influential person was Nana Lou, the grandmother who raised her. Latisha told us about a college professor who changed her life by recognizing her artistic talent. I had no idea she ran a thriving jewelry design business. Nora had us in tears when she told the story of her big brother who protected her from the ravages of their abusive father.

The stories continued, each more powerful than the next. By the time everyone had finished, even the most stoic members of the group were wiping tears from their eyes.

I waited a couple of minutes until everyone had regained their composure. Then I posed the real question—the most important question of all.

"We've had the opportunity to listen to some amazing stories here today," I said. "We heard 12 stories about people who made a difference in our lives. Even though each person was unique, they all had one trait in common. What was it?" I asked.

There was a long silence, and finally Judy raised her hand. She rarely said much, but when she did, we all listened. "I guess what they all had in common was that they were very generous. Each one took the time to listen to us. They recognized our value."

She paused. As she placed her hand over her heart, she said softly, "Each person had a generous heart."

That was the day everything changed. The fighting melons became a team.

Aha! #17

**OUR STORIES
CONNECT US WITH
EACH OTHER.**

CHAPTER 9

Generous Hearts Make a Difference

Over the next few weeks my team inched up in the rankings. Instead of dead last, by week four we were in the middle of the pack. Our weekly meetings were actually fun. We brainstormed ways to reduce errors and improve our scores. We set small goals, and we met them most of the time. Even when we didn't, we felt we'd made progress. We were actually a *team*.

Our team no longer went by the name of the Generators. On their own, the team decided that they needed a new name to match their new attitude. At the start of one of our weekly meetings Latisha unveiled the new team logo she had designed. It featured a bright red heart and just below it were the words "Make a Difference"—a reminder to us all that generous hearts make a difference.

I almost cried.

My months as team leader flew by. I was incredibly busy and surprisingly well organized. The more I practiced being open and expecting the best, the more good things came my way. I was reminded how much easier my life was when I practiced being patient and kind—with myself and with others. I reveled in my newfound confidence.

I had my share of setbacks and disappointments. But instead of being discouraged when things didn't go as I had planned or as I had hoped, I accepted it. Instead of wasting my energy feeling sorry for myself or being angry at somebody, I focused on finding opportunities in the unexpected. I was surprised to discover that things always worked out in the end, even if it wasn't as I had planned.

Isabel and I got into the habit of greeting each other with an open hand and a smile. I'm sure it was gratifying for her to see how happy I had become. I hoped that someday I could do for others what she had done for me. Until recently, I had considered my Uncle John the most influential person in my life. I hoped he wouldn't mind sharing that honor with Isabel.

Isabel and I either talked or corresponded by e-mail a couple of times a week. My e-mails chronicled my victories as well as my disappointments. Periodically, I'd tell her how disheartened I was when something didn't go the way I had hoped. I could count on her to help me to step back and see *what is* and to have a SODA.

There were times when I didn't need to tell her I was feeling overwhelmed. She knew. That's when a napkin magically appeared on my chair.

I sat down one day and sent her an e-mail updating her on the many "aha!" moments I had had.

. . .

MY LIST OF "AHA!s"

Aha! #1: I will always have problems.

Aha! #2: It's not about me.

Aha! #3: Problems can be gifts in disguise.

Aha! #4: Just sit there. Do nothing.

Aha! #5: There is no such thing as a difficult situation.

Aha! #6: When all else fails, have a SODA.

Aha! #7: Withholding judgment allows me to observe *what is*.

Aha! #8: The nicer I am to myself, the nicer I am to others.

Aha! #9: A simple apology works wonders.

Aha! #10: The less I talk, the more I learn.

Aha! #11: People harmonize when they are tuned to the same frequency.
When I tried to figure out why people were smiling at me for "no reason," I discovered that there really was a reason. They were responding to my positive feelings with positive feelings of their own.

Aha! #12: Great supervisors follow the Golden Rule and do the right thing.
As a team leader I have found that when I follow these two simple rules I can't go wrong.

Aha! #13: Spreading my wings is the only way to fly.
I am so glad I didn't let my fear of flying—trying something I hadn't done before—get in my way. The little nudge that Jake gave me was all I needed to take a chance and say yes to Lucy's offer to be a team leader for six months.

Aha! #14: Give a little. Get a lot.
Once I made a conscious effort to be more generous and understanding of others, good things happened. It was as if I were being rewarded for doing the right thing.

Aha! #15: Remember, we all share the same vine.
The story of the fighting melons helped the members of my team realize that they needed to stop bickering and work in harmony.

Aha! #16: United we stand. Divided we fall.
My team finally realized that the only way they could be successful is if they focused on the same goals.

Aha! #17: Our stories connect us with each other.

The best thing about telling our stories was that it helped us recognize how much we had in common. Our stories helped us connect with one another. We could see that we weren't so different after all.

. . .

I was feeling too good and too happy to allow myself to become miserable again. I knew that if I didn't keep visual reminders around that it would be just a matter of time before I reverted back to the old me. I taped one list of "aha!s" in my cube and another on my bathroom mirror at home. I framed the first napkin that Isabel gave me. It sat right next to my computer.

It took almost a year before somebody caught me unplugging. I was in the abandoned office one morning and had just drifted into that quiet place in my mind when the door opened. It was Kari. One by one she sifted through each box of files until she worked her way to where I was sitting.

"Oh! I'm so sorry," she apologized. "I didn't know anybody was in here." She paused. "Olivia, are you okay?" she said softly.

"Oh, I'm fine. I just come in here to get some quiet time by myself. It helps me unplug from all the craziness out there. I was just about finished anyway," I replied.

She grinned. "Unplug? You do it, too?" she exclaimed.

I nodded and laughed to myself. Sweet Isabel strikes again!

I asked her when she found time in the day to unplug. "On the bus," she replied. "I have a 40-minute bus ride to and from work every day. I settle into my seat and unplug right there on the bus.

"I was a little nervous at first, thinking the people around me would find it strange that I was sitting there with my eyes closed. Nobody noticed. Everybody was too busy doing their own thing. I unplug both on the way to the office and on the way home. You know, it's hard to explain how it works or even why it works. All I know is that learning to unplug has changed my whole outlook on life."

"I know exactly what you mean. It's changed me, too," I replied. "I know it's working because on the days when I don't unplug, I don't have as much patience."

"I've been thinking about this a lot," Kari said. "What I've figured out is that the only thing that is real is what is happening right here, right now, at this moment. When I recognized that things by themselves have no meaning until *I* place a meaning on them, it all began to make sense."

She pointed to the box next to me. "Take this box, for example. It is a box of files, similar to all of the other boxes in here. It's not better than the other boxes. It's just a box. Since I'm looking for a specific file, I'm the one who decides whether it's the 'right' box or the 'wrong' box. The box itself just is what it is."

I knew the answer, but I asked the question anyway. "Was it Isabel who shared the idea of unplugging with you?"

"Why yes!" Kari exclaimed. "Matter of fact, she has passed along the idea to several of us. It is such a personal thing that none of us goes around talking about it. Sometimes a familiar word just creeps into the conversation. I know I've found a fellow unplugger when they talk about stopping to see *what is* or when they comment on how good it feels to unplug from the stresses of their job for a few minutes."

I knew the answer to the next question, too. "By any chance, did Isabel draw you a picture of two circles and a space in between—on a napkin?"

"Yep! You too, huh?" She giggled. "I suppose she hands you a napkin whenever she sees you getting stressed out?"

I nodded.

On the way back to my cube, I passed Lucy's office. She waved me in. "Olivia! Just the person I was looking for. Come on in and shut the door."

I wondered what I had done.

"Olivia, I want to compliment you on what you've done with your team. Once they learned how to work together they really took off. You added just the spark they needed.

"Your team's success seems to have created a ripple effect," she smiled. "The other teams have been spurred on to try even harder. As a result, our overall performance has improved dramatically."

Lucy was actually beaming. "We have fewer errors. We are answering calls more quickly, so customers rarely have to hold for more than a few seconds. Best of all, our scores for customer satisfaction have never been higher."

I told her that was nice to hear. "Thanks for the compliment, but it was my team that did all the work. Plus, I think we had an advantage. We have a lot of talented people."

She quickly dismissed that idea. "Olivia, you are way too modest! Sure, you have good people, but so do the other teams. Your team has succeeded because you have been able to bring out the best in each person. Take Nikki, for example."

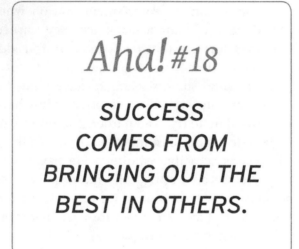

Aha! #18

*SUCCESS
COMES FROM
BRINGING OUT THE
BEST IN OTHERS.*

Miss Grumpy had become our team's Most Valuable Player. When Nikki pointed out that the reason we were doing so poorly was because the new hires were making too many errors, she was right. However, the people weren't the problem. They were certainly smart enough. The problem was the training, or in this case, a lack of it.

Nikki took the initiative to do a little research and found the answer. The training manager had needed to trim his budget. So he decided that he could save some money if he reduced the number of weeks that new employees spent in training.

Nikki went beyond pointing out the problem; she came up with a creative solution. First she identified the gaps in the new service reps' initial training by interviewing the trainees and the rest of the team. She didn't stop there. She organized a team effort to create our own "skill gap" training class.

I don't know how she did it, but she persuaded her teammates to give up two of their precious Saturdays to come in to conduct training for the new hires. Each of the experienced reps presented information on the area of the job that they knew best.

The additional training did the trick. Our error rate plummeted. Nikki gained a lot of confidence from the experience and discovered she had a knack for doing training. Other teams heard about

Aha! #19

WINNERS DON'T JUST POINT OUT PROBLEMS. THEY FIX THEM.

her and asked her for help. Before long, she was on the shortlist to fill a job in the Training Department.

As it turned out, HR hired somebody with a degree in staff development. Nikki was disappointed. But instead of getting angry and claiming she wasn't treated fairly, which she probably would have done in earlier days, she made the decision to finish her education. Nikki enrolled in a weekend college program.

Lucy continued, "Well, I have some news," she said proudly. "As you probably know, Stu, the customer care manager, is planning to retire. Well, Olivia, I applied and was offered the job yesterday."

"You accepted, I hope?" I said, thinking that decision had to be a no-brainer.

"I did accept the position. I'm going to be the new manager of customer care." Lucy replied. "I'm pretty excited about it—and a little scared, frankly. The position will be a stretch for me, but I think I'm ready. I'll never know if I can meet the challenge unless I give it a try.

"I'd appreciate it if you didn't tell anybody else quite yet. I'd rather everybody find out when the official announcement is made on Monday. But I wanted to tell you now because I'd like you to think about applying for the supervisor's job. It would be a good career move for you."

Lucy looked at me, expecting an answer. I must have had a deer-in-the-headlights look on my face. "All I ask is that you think about it. If you decide to apply, you'll want to talk with HR as soon as possible."

We were interrupted by an urgent knock on Lucy's door. A service rep was visibly upset. Two more were waiting in line behind her. That could be my life as a supervisor, I thought. I took my leave and promised to think about her offer over the weekend and let her know on Monday.

On the drive home, I thought about Lucy's comment that the supervisor's job would be "a good career move" for me. *What career?* I laughed. Until I started working at Mighty Power, all I cared about was a regular paycheck. My definition of success was having a decent-paying office job that had health insurance and a retirement plan.

Building a career in business had never been on my radar. In college, I bounced from one major to another. First it was English literature, next it was art history, then psychology, and finally sociology. I arrived at that major only after realizing that I had more classes in that subject than any other.

My experiences since starting at Mighty Power had got me thinking less about a paycheck and more about the possibility of building a career. In fact, now that I had a more positive outlook on life and felt more confident, I could see that my future was full of possibilities. Who knew? I could start moving up in the company and even be a supervisor someday.

It looked like that "someday" had arrived.

CHAPTER 10

The Napkin, the Melon, and the Monkey

Friday nights were reserved as "date night" for Jake and me. We would catch a movie at the local mall and go out to dinner afterward. Since our tastes in movies were different (he liked live action and I preferred romantic comedies), we either negotiated a compromise or took turns choosing what to see. One thing we did agree on was where we would go for dinner.

Gino's was a family-owned restaurant in our neighborhood. The atmosphere was casual and the food bordered on divine. Gino, the proprietor, looked like every Italian maître d' you've ever seen in the movies. Charming, gracious, and attentive to detail, he was the perfect host. He'd always greet Jake by name and refer to me as "lovely Olivia," just like my Uncle John used to.

That Friday night, I waited until we were seated at our favorite table to tell Jake about Lucy's promotion and my new opportunity. I had been tempted to share my news in the car on the way to the movie, but decided I'd wait for the right moment. I was sure he'd be delighted. I couldn't have been more wrong.

"Jake, I thought you'd be happy about the possibility of my being promoted to supervisor," I said, trying to hide my disappointment. Tears welled up in my eyes.

"Sweetie, I am happy for you," he said softly. "I'm confident you would do a great job as a supervisor. But—"

"But what?" I blurted.

Jake hesitated, searching for just the right words, "Olivia, I have come to really enjoy the new you. You are so much happier. You are so much easier to live with. I just don't want you to go back to the way you were. I'm afraid that as a supervisor you will be under a lot more stress. I know how you get when you're stressed out. We all suffer. If Mom's not happy, nobody's happy."

Hurt and angry, I struck back, and before I knew it, I was accusing him of being threatened by my success. He said that wasn't it at all. He tried to convince me. I started to cry. We left our dinners half-eaten and paid the bill. As we were walking out, he tried to put his arm around my shoulder, but I shook him off.

Instead of getting into our car, I stormed past it and walked the five blocks home. My mind was racing. Emotions ricocheted from raging anger to paralyzing fear and then back again. By the time I arrived home, I still wasn't calm enough to face my husband.

I sat on the back steps in the dark. The air was cool. I felt the tears drying on my cheeks. *Why am I feeling so angry and so afraid?* I wondered. *Is Jake right? Are his fears justified? Will a high-stress job result in my going back to being crabby and miserable? Will I crumble under the pressure of being a supervisor? Am I doomed to be perpetually stressed out and screwed up?*

Eventually I managed to calm down. I concentrated on slowing my breathing. "Breathe in . . . slowly . . . breathe out . . . slowly," I whispered.

Little by little my thoughts slowed down, too. I observed them floating in and gently floating out. I stopped to see *what is*.

If I did get the job, which was a big "if," I would have to deal with new situations every day. I had learned that while I couldn't control what happened to me, I could control how I reacted. As long as I continued to unplug each day and follow the process that I had learned—to stop my emotions long enough to observe *what is* and then decide how to act—I would be okay. I would be more than just okay. I would continue to be happy.

I found Jake seated at the kitchen table, staring into his cup of coffee, looking wounded and worried. I slipped in quietly beside him and placed my hand on his. "Jake, I love you," I whispered.

"I love you too, sweetie. I hope—"

I interrupted him. "You don't need to explain. As a husband and father, I can understand your concern. And frankly, I don't blame you. I don't want to go back to the old me, either."

He looked relieved.

"Jake, I've made my decision. I am going to apply for this job. There is no guarantee even if I do apply for it that I will get it. I just know that if I pass up this opportunity, I will kick myself later. As you say, I have to be in the game in order to win."

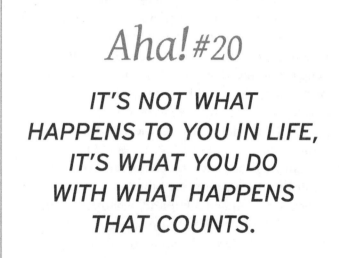

Aha! #20

IT'S NOT WHAT HAPPENS TO YOU IN LIFE, IT'S WHAT YOU DO WITH WHAT HAPPENS THAT COUNTS.

My sweet husband put his arms around me and whispered, "Baby, I love you more today than ever. You are just beginning to see what I've known all along—what an exceptional woman you really are." I felt myself melting deeper into his arms.

"The changes you have made over the last year have shown you what can happen when you decide to get out of your own way. Honey, if you just keep on doing what you've been doing, there will be no stopping you. I have faith that you will give it your best shot and take care of yourself."

That's my Jake, always the wind beneath my wings.

Lucy's promotion to customer care manager was officially announced Monday morning. That afternoon I contacted HR and became a candidate for the job of customer care supervisor. I was informed that one of the first things Mr. Mathwig had done when he took over as CEO was to institute a more rigorous hiring process. He had made it clear to HR that they would need to fill every job opening with the "best and the brightest." The bar had been raised.

Instead of taking a week or two, the screening process would take two months. There was no shortage of candidates from outside the company.

The ad in Sunday's paper generated over 50 résumés in the first week.

I had read in the local paper recently that a lot of new companies were locating in our area. Potential employers didn't decide to come here because we had the best weather in the country—far from it. Our long, cold winters were legendary. But we had a labor force known for its conscientious work ethic. More companies meant more customer service departments and a larger pool of supervisors that would be interested in applying for this job.

The competition from within was stiff too. Several qualified people applied, but the one I was the most concerned about was Luis, one of our department's team leaders. When it came to experience, he had me beat. My paltry six months paled in comparison to his three years as a team leader.

Luckily for me, the aptitude test I took as part of the screening process showed that I had the right qualities to be a successful supervisor in a call center. I hoped that my test scores, along with the interviews, would offset my lack of experience. In fact, I was banking on it.

I thought I was doing pretty well juggling the rigors of the selection process and everything else in my life. Until the morning my kids gave me a reality check.

Feeling rushed, I scolded Nate and Natalie for not moving fast enough to catch their bus. Natalie, thinking I was out of earshot, whispered to her brother, "Uh-oh, Mommy's got her crabby pants on again." Maybe foreseeing even more unpleasant mornings in the future, Nate sighed, "Yeah, I know."

Maybe Jake was right to worry! I thought. *I am losing my grip on things.*

When I got to work, there was another not-so-subtle reminder that I was slipping back into my pre-unplugging behavior. A napkin was waiting for me on my chair. So I called Isabel and asked her to have lunch. It was a beautiful day, so we decided to sit on a bench in the park across the street.

"I'm afraid I'm slipping back into my old ways, Isabel. Getting this supervisor's job has taken over my life! I'm a woman possessed! No sooner do I get over one hurdle in the hiring process, when I begin stressing about what I need to do to get over the next one. The more I try to control things the more out of control I feel," I confessed.

"And since when did you have control?" she chuckled. I had unplugged only once in the last two weeks. "This has taught me once again how important my daily unplugging is to keeping my head on straight."

As if on cue, the woman with a story for every occasion delivered another gem. "Olivia, I have a story that may help you see your situation more clearly. It's one of my favorites," she said softly.

"Trapping and selling wild monkeys was a lucrative business in Mexico at one time. Poachers would capture them by placing containers in the forest with a piece of sweet coconut meat. The container had a hole barely large enough for the monkey to put its hand in and grip the coconut. But if the monkey tried to withdraw its hand, it found that as long as it kept a grip on the food it was trapped. If it let go of what it wanted, it was free."

My wise friend looked at me expectantly.

"I get it," I laughed. "It appears that those monkeys and I have a lot in common! The more the monkey tried to hang on, the more trapped it became. If it could just let go of what it wanted, it would be free again."

Isabel smiled, "How does that apply to your current situation?"

"The more obsessed I am about getting this job, the more trapped I feel. I keep telling myself that life will be better once I get that new job. But down deep I know that my life won't be significantly better. It will just be different, that's all." I continued, "I'm creating my own mental anguish by worrying so much about the end result. I am back to trying to control things that are way beyond my control."

"Indeed," Isabel replied. "You will see that the less attached you are to the outcome, the more powerful you will feel. I guarantee that when you focus less on what may or may not happen in the future and more on remaining in the here and now, you will be happier.

"My advice is to do the best you can and after that, let it go. The decision about whether you get the supervisor's job is not up to you, so the outcome is now out of your hands."

After our talk, I resumed my daily unplugging and regained my balance. When I returned to being nicer to myself, I was nicer to everyone else. I apologized to Nate and Natalie for being such a crab that morning. They were back to being happy, too.

I began to apply the lesson from the monkey's story right away. Emotionally I arrived at a place where I was okay with whatever happened. Sure, I'd be disappointed if I didn't get the supervisor's job, but I'd accept that it wasn't the right time for me to be a supervisor.

The selection process for the supervisor's job dragged on for another three weeks. First interviews led to second interviews. Eventually, the field of

Aha! #21

REAL FREEDOM COMES FROM LETTING GO OF THE OUTCOME.

candidates was whittled down to two finalists—Luis and me.

When the day came for the big decision, I was ready. It was the director of HR who placed the call. "Good morning, Olivia, this is Naomi. Listen, I just wanted to let you know we have made a decision."

I took a deep breath.

"As you know, we were fortunate to have several terrific candidates to choose from. It was difficult, but in the end we determined that there was one candidate who clearly stood out."

She paused.

"Olivia, I'd like to officially offer you the position of customer care supervisor."

The rest of the day was a blur. Shortly after I hung up, Lucy arrived to congratulate me. A steady stream of coworkers stopped by to wish me well once the rumor mill kicked into full gear.

Even Luis stopped by. He said that while he was disappointed, he was glad I was the one who got the job. I appreciated his generous offer to help me in any way he could. As Coach Jake liked to say when one of the twins lost a soccer game, "Anybody can handle winning a game. The real champion is the one who can lose gracefully."

Before I had a chance to call him, a big bouquet of roses arrived with a card that read, "Congratulations on the home run. All my love, Jake."

And then there was Isabel. She arrived the next day with three beautifully wrapped boxes. I could tell by the look on her face that these were no ordinary gifts.

I opened the smallest box first. It contained an industrial-looking napkin dispenser filled to the brim. "So I can always remind myself to have a SODA," I laughed.

Package number two was large and very heavy. This one contained a big ripe watermelon.

Knowing what was in the first two boxes, I should have guessed what was in the third. Box number three contained a smiling stuffed monkey.

"A napkin, a melon, and a monkey," I laughed. Thank you, Isabel. I'll treasure them always."

She paused for a moment and took my hand in hers. "I hope you do. Now that you have them, I trust you will pass them on to others."

Just as she reached the door to leave, she stopped and turned around. With a twinkle in her eye, she whispered, "That's the way it works, you know."

Aha! #22

GENEROUS HEARTS MAKE A DIFFERENCE.

OLIVIA'S LIST OF "AHA!s"

Aha! #1: I will always have problems.

Aha! #2: It's not about me.

Aha! #3: Problems can be gifts in disguise.

Aha! #4: Just sit there. Do nothing.

Aha! #5: There is no such thing as a difficult situation.

Aha! #6: When all else fails, have a SODA.

Aha! #7: Withholding judgment allows me to observe *what is*.

Aha! #8: The nicer I am to myself, the nicer I am to others.

Aha! #9: A simple apology works wonders.

Aha! #10: The less I talk, the more I learn.

Aha! #11: People harmonize when they are tuned to the same frequency.

Aha! #12: Great supervisors follow the Golden Rule and do the right thing.

Aha! #13: Spreading my wings is the only way to fly.

Aha! #14: Give a little. Get a lot.

Aha! #15: Remember, we all share the same vine.

Aha! #16: United we stand. Divided we fall.

Aha! #17: Our stories connect us with each other.

Aha! #18: Success comes from bringing out the best in others.

Aha! #19: Winners don't just point out problems. They fix them.

Aha! #20: It's not what happens to you in life, it's what you do with what happens that counts.

Aha! #21: Real freedom comes from letting go of the outcome.

Aha! #22: Generous hearts make a difference.

ACKNOWLEDGMENTS

If I could recall the name of the woman who asked me, 15 years ago, how to handle angry, abusive customers, I would extend a big thank-you to her. Fueled by her question and at my daughter Megan Fluegel's suggestion, I decided to write this book. I am grateful to Ellen Keller, Dale and Barbara Ver Kuilen, and Ricky Peterson for helping me hone my ideas. Thanks also to my friends for cheering me on every step of the way.

I owe a debt of gratitude to the 150 customer service representatives, supervisors, and managers who read the manuscript and gave valuable feedback. Thanks to my clients Ed Karpinski, Vern Edwards, Jim Smith, Tim Burke, Joe Calabrese, Juan Garza, and Regina Hogan for introducing early versions of the book to their employees.

Encouraged by the positive response to the story, in 2006 I published the book myself. Thanks to Kari Alberg for the beautiful design of that original book; and thanks to my brother, Tom Roster, my sister, Susan Fotos, and her husband, Stephen Fotos, for their unwavering support at every turn.

I am grateful to Donna Alvado, Judy Heinen, Pam Zaniboni, Deb Patterson, and Carrie Kelly, who piloted the use of *The Napkin, The Melon & The Monkey* to train their staff. Thanks also to my colleagues who spread the word about the book, particularly Becky Amble, Audray Lewis-Adams, and Ashley Baptiste. And I owe a special thanks to the hundreds of managers who championed the use of the book to make a difference within their organizations.

I am grateful to my agent, Joelle Delbourgo, for her belief in the universal message of the book and her wise counsel. I thank Patty Gift at Hay House for acquiring the book and being so wise and kind. Thanks also to my entire Hay House team for smoothing the way for this first-time author.

ABOUT THE AUTHOR

Barbara Burke is an internationally known consultant, speaker, and author specializing in the "people side" of customer service management. At the core of her philosophy is the belief that exceptional customer service is only possible when the employees providing the service feel valued and engaged. In the last 25 years, thousands of front-line employees and their leaders have benefited from her innovative training programs. Her clients include Honeywell, Progress Energy, Alltel, Microsoft, Estée Lauder, Target Corporation, Portland General Electric, the State of Minnesota, the State of Pennsylvania, Procter & Gamble, Cox Communications, Vertex, Time-Warner, and Austin Energy.

To invite Barbara to speak to your group, visit **www.barbaraburke.com** or call (507) 663-7232 for more information about her inspirational keynotes and seminars. Managers interested in resources for integrating the powerful ideas from *The Napkin, The Melon & The Monkey* into their organization can visit **www.napkinmelonmonkey.com**.

We hope you enjoyed this Hay House book. If you'd like to receive our online catalog featuring additional information on Hay House books and products, or if you'd like to find out more about the Hay Foundation, please contact:

Hay House, Inc., P.O. Box 5100, Carlsbad, CA 92018-5100

(760) 431-7695 or **(800) 654-5126**
(760) 431-6948 (fax) or **(800) 650-5115 (fax)**
www.hayhouse.com® • **www.hayfoundation.org**

. . .

Published and distributed in Australia by:
Hay House Australia Pty. Ltd., 18/36 Ralph St., Alexandria NSW
2015 • *Phone:* 612-9669-4299 • *Fax:* 612-9669-4144
www.hayhouse.com.au

Published and distributed in the United Kingdom by:
Hay House UK, Ltd., 292B Kensal Rd., London W10 5BE
Phone: 44-20-8962-1230 • *Fax:* 44-20-8962-1239
www.hayhouse.co.uk

Published and distributed in the Republic of South Africa by:
Hay House SA (Pty), Ltd., P.O. Box 990, Witkoppen 2068
Phone/Fax: 27-11-467-8904 • info@hayhouse.co.za
www.hayhouse.co.za

Published in India by:
Hay House Publishers India,
Muskaan Complex, Plot No. 3, B-2, Vasant Kunj, New Delhi
110 070 • *Phone:* 91-11-4176-1620 • *Fax:* 91-11-4176-1630
www.hayhouse.co.in

Distributed in Canada by:
Raincoast, 9050 Shaughnessy St., Vancouver, B.C. V6P 6E5
Phone: (604) 323-7100 • *Fax:* (604) 323-2600
www.raincoast.com

. . .

Take Your Soul on a Vacation

Visit **www.HealYourLife.com®** to regroup, recharge,
and reconnect with your own magnificence. Featuring
blogs, mind-body-spirit news, and life-changing
wisdom from Louise Hay and friends.

Visit **www.HealYourLife.com** today!